W Leela

By Jyotsna Sreenivasan
Illustrated by Siri Weber Feeney

Weird Leela
Copyright © Wright Group/McGraw-Hill
By Jyotsna Sreenivasan
Illustrated by Siri Weber Feeney

SUNSHINE™ is a trademark of The McGraw-Hill Companies Inc.

All rights reserved. No part of this publication may be reproduced or distributed in any form or by any means, or stored in a database or retrieval system, without the prior written consent of The McGraw-Hill Companies, Inc., including, but not limited to, network or other electronic storage or transmission, or broadcast for distance learning.

Send all inquiries to:
Wright Group/McGraw-Hill
P.O. Box 812960
Chicago, IL 60681

Printed in China through Colorcraft Ltd, Hong Kong

10 9 8 7

ISBN: 0-322-04493-6
ISBN: 0-322-04589-4 (6-pack)

Contents

CHAPTER 1: My Weird Grandmother ... 5

CHAPTER 2: The Special Treat 9

CHAPTER 3: My Very Unlucky Day 15

CHAPTER 4: A Strange Foreign Girl 23

CHAPTER 5: Not Indian Anymore 29

CHAPTER 6: The Third Eye 37

Indian Pronunciation Guide 48

CHAPTER 1
My Weird Grandmother

"Hang up the phone, Leela!" I hear my dad calling from the front hallway. "We'll be late to meet the plane."

"I'm almost done!" I yell back. I'm talking to my best friend, Anushri. "Are you one thousand-percent sure you don't want to come with us?" I ask her again.

My dad and I are going to pick up my grandmother at the airport. She's coming all the way from Bangalore, India, to stay with us for five months.

"Yes, I'm two thousand-percent sure!" Anushri says. "I'm busy today."

I know Anushri's not busy. I think she might be jealous. Her grandmother's too sick to travel from India to visit her.

"Leela, I'm leaving!" Dad calls.

"I gotta go. Bye!" I hang up the phone and run out to the car.

Pretty soon we're in the Cleveland airport, watching people rushing out of gate 29. Finally, I see my grandmother coming through the doorway.

"Ajji!" I shout. *Ajji* is the word for *grandmother* in the Kannada language. Ajji hugs me. As we walk, I give Ajji the drawing I made to show her some differences about life in America. Ajji's never been here before, but I've visited India for two summers already, so I know a lot of the things that are different in America. I drew a picture of Anushri and me wearing shorts and having a picnic with strawberries, blueberries, and peanut-butter sandwiches. Indian people don't eat those foods. They eat fruits like mangos, guavas, and bananas and they take yogurt rice to picnics. And girls in India don't wear shorts. They usually wear dresses, or sometimes a long skirt called a *langa*.

As we walk past the bathroom, I see the most popular girl in my class, Crystal, standing against a wall.

"Hi, Crystal!" I shout and wave. "Meet my grandmother!" I grab Ajji's hand and drag her toward Crystal.

Ajji says, "Nice to meet you." Crystal doesn't say anything. She looks at Ajji. Ajji's black-and-gray hair is pulled back into a bun. She has a large, round red dot in the middle of her forehead and a nose stud with a red jewel in it. Ajji is wearing a light blue cloth called a sari that is wrapped and pleated around her, a pair of Indian sandals called *chappals,* and toe rings on each foot.

My dad calls, "Let's go!" and Ajji walks away. I wave good-bye to Crystal. As I turn to follow Ajji, I hear Crystal mutter, "Weird!" just under her breath.

I just stand there. I feel like I've been slapped. Does Crystal think Ajji is weird? And if she thinks Ajji is weird, does she think I'm weird, too?

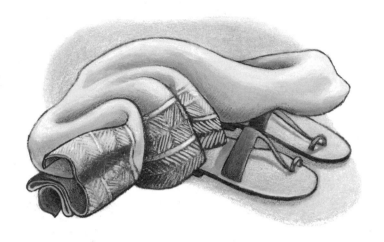

CHAPTER 2
The Special Treat

The next morning, just as I'm heading out the door with my book bag, Ajji comes down the steps into the front hallway.

"Where does your bus pick you up?" Ajji asks.

"Just around the corner." I open the front door.

"In that case, I'll walk with you," Ajji says. She puts on her chappals and throws a shawl around her shoulders.

What if the kids at the bus stop act like Crystal did, when they see Ajji? I'll die of embarrassment.

"No, Ajji. You don't have to do that."

"It's nothing at all. I love to take long walks. This is only a short distance."

"No, really, Ajji. It's okay."

But Ajji is already headed out the door.

I have to do something! I shut the front door, run past my mom in the kitchen and out the back door. I run all the way to the bus stop, going the other way around the block. Fortunately, the bus arrives just as I do, and I climb aboard and sit down next to Anushri. As the bus pulls away from the curb, I see Ajji walking toward the bus. Ajji waves. I look away, but Anushri waves back.

Someone behind us says, "Hey, is that your grandmother?"

I turn to see Nicholas, a boy in my class, pointing out the window. "She arrived yesterday, right?"

I forgot that I told my entire class about Ajji's visit!

"What happened to her forehead?" Nicholas asked. "It looks like it's bleeding."

I don't answer. I just sink lower in my seat.

"What's wrong, Leela?" Anushri asks. "Why didn't you wave to your grandmother?"

"Shh!" I whisper. "Anushri, everyone thinks Ajji is weird!" And I tell her all about Crystal.

"So what?" Anushri says. "You should be happy your grandmother's here. I wish my grandmother could be here to walk me to the bus stop."

When we get to school, Anushri goes to her classroom and I go to mine. No one says anything about Ajji all day—not even Crystal. Right before school ends, my teacher, Ms. Hamilton, asks the class to be quiet. Then she says, "We'll have a special treat this week."

I wonder what the special treat could be. Maybe it's an ice-cream social. We had one of those a few months ago. Or maybe it's a pizza party. I love pizza!

Ms. Hamilton continues, "We all know that Leela's grandmother has come from India for a visit."

What did my grandmother have to do with a special treat?

"And I just learned that Leela's grandmother has agreed to give our class a presentation about life in India on Thursday afternoon!"

Oh, no! While everyone else is picking up their book bags and putting on their jackets, I just sit in my seat. How will I ever live through this?

CHAPTER 3
My Very Unlucky Day

On Thursday morning, I go downstairs in my pajamas. Mom and Ajji are both in the kitchen, putting brown *gulab jamun* balls into sugar syrup. Ajji is bringing them to school today for her presentation. They are my favorite Indian dessert, but right now looking at them makes my stomach hurt.

"Mom," I groan. "I think I'm sick."

"Sick?" Mom feels my forehead. "You don't feel warm and you look fine to me.

You probably just need some breakfast. Eat your cereal."

On the bus, Anushri says, "You're so lucky that your grandmother's coming to school today!"

"You mean unlucky," I mutter.

Ajji is coming at two o'clock. All morning I feel sick to my stomach. And after lunch, I keep turning around to look at the clock on the back wall of the classroom. As the minutes tick by, the butterflies in my stomach grow worse and worse.

Finally there is a knock at the door. Ms. Hamilton opens it and in comes Ajji. Some kids stare at her. Other kids look at me and smile. I know they must be laughing at me. I wish I could disappear.

Behind Ajji, I see my father come in, too! He's carrying a slide projector and the box of slides from our last trip to

India. And behind him is my mother holding the pan full of gulab jamun. Dad waves to me. I try to smile, but I feel like crying.

"Leela, would you like to introduce our guests?" Ms. Hamilton asks.

I shake my head.

"All right." Ms. Hamilton introduces Ajji and my parents herself.

Then she turns out the lights and Ajji starts the slide show. A picture of a crowded Indian street lights up the screen.

"In India, everyone shares the road," Ajji says. "Cars, buses, lorries, cycles. You will find them all on an Indian road."

"What's a lorry?" Lucy asks.

Ajji looks confused.

"It's a truck," Dad says. "In India we call them lorries."

I can't believe that Ajji doesn't even know the American word for such a common thing!

Next is a picture of an *autoriksha*. "This is a very unusual vehicle," Ajji says. "It's like a taxi but it has only three wheels. The driver sits up front, and the passengers sit in back. There is a roof but no doors, so if it is raining, you can still get wet!"

Then Ajji shows a picture of my aunt's kitchen. The walls are a brownish yellow color, and the countertops are dark black.

"That looks like a very small kitchen," Crystal says. "And dirty, too."

Ajji laughs. "It's much smaller than your American kitchens. But it is actually very clean, just not so white as your kitchens here."

After more slides, Ajji asks if there are any questions.

"How come you speak English so well?" asks Nicholas.

"Many educated people in India speak English," Ajji explains. "It is one of our official languages. There are over a dozen different languages in India."

I'm glad everyone's looking at Ajji, and not at me. Then I see my mom coming up to my desk. She whispers,

"Come and help me serve the gulab jamuns."

So I have to get up and walk around the class to give each kid a bowl with one gulab jamun in it. Of course everyone stares at me.

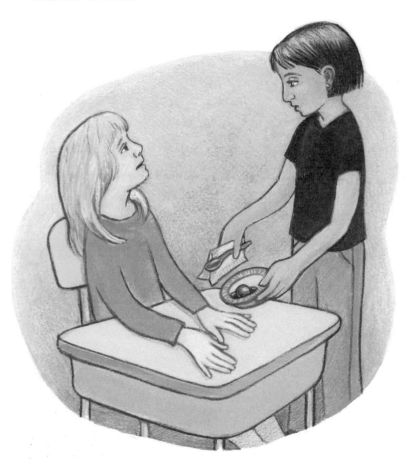

When I get to Crystal's desk, she sticks out her tongue. *"Eeww!* This looks gross," she whines.

"It tastes like pancakes, only better," I whisper. I feel like shouting at her, but if I do, I think I might start to cry.

CHAPTER 4
A Strange Foreign Girl

When my alarm rings the next morning, I roll over and pull the covers over my head. I wonder if I can convince Mom to let me stay home today.

But before I can get up to ask her, Mom comes into my room and sits on my bed. "I have something to tell you," she says. I sit up.

"Anushri's mom called me late last night. Anushri's grandmother died yesterday."

"Oh, no! I know how much Anushri loved her grandmother!" I say.

"Anushri's mom left for India this morning," Mom says. "Anushri will be staying with us while her mother is gone. I know you will be a good friend to Anushri and help her through this very difficult time."

When I get to the bus stop, Anushri doesn't even look up at me. I don't know what to do, so I just say, "I'm really sorry to hear about your grandmother." She smiles a little bit, but I can tell she's trying not to cry.

All morning I try not to talk to anyone else or even look at anyone. I'm afraid that if I look at other kids, or talk to them, they'll say something about how strange I am. But no one says anything.

At recess, I meet Anushri by the monkey bars. I can see from her red eyes that she has been crying, but she seems a little bit better. "After school will you come over and help me pack?" she asks as she climbs on the monkey bars.

"Sure," I say. I'm glad there's at least one other person in my school who doesn't think I'm weird.

Just then I hear a loud whooping sound. Over to the right, on the grass, there's a whole group of kids. That's where the noise is coming from. We jump down and go see what they're all looking at.

As we get near, all the kids turn around and look at us. They are laughing. Then I see Nicholas and Crystal running around in the middle of the circle of kids. They have big red dots on their foreheads. Crystal even has a red dot on

her nose. And they're making sounds with their hands against their mouths, like kids do when they want to pretend to be American Indians. When Crystal sees me she calls loudly, "Hey look! It's Weird Leela! Weird Leela!" The kids laugh even harder.

I turn around and run as fast as I can to the corner of the school building. I stand facing the wall so no one can see the tears in my eyes.

Anushri comes running up after me.

"Leela, those kids just don't understand. They don't know anything about you or your grandmother. They don't even know the difference between American Indians and Indian Americans. Who cares about them," she says. "Come on, let's play."

But I care. I wish my grandmother had never come from India. Before she came, no one made fun of me. I was Leela, a normal girl who happened to have brown skin. But now I'm Weird Leela, a strange girl from a faraway foreign land.

CHAPTER 5
Not Indian Anymore

"What do you mean, you're not coming?" Anushri asks. "How can you not come? It's in your own house!"

"I'm just not."

We are both up in my bedroom. It's Sunday afternoon, and Anushri is getting dressed for the *bhajan* group that is gathering at my house. Every month, a whole bunch of my parents' friends get together to sing religious songs called bhajans.

Anushri puts on a green langa with gold leaves embroidered all over it and a green blouse. She slips stacks of green glass bangles onto both arms. She picks up a gold-colored barrette and says, "I'm going to ask Ajji if she will help me with my hair."

Anushri's only been staying with us for a few days, but already my ajji is her ajji! Well, she can have her! I don't care.

All day long, Anushri has been helping Ajji and my mom get ready for bhajan. She went outside and cut daffodils to put in a vase in front of the pictures of gods and goddesses. She helped Ajji make cotton wicks for the tall brass lamps that will be lit in front of the altar. She even helped my mom vacuum the carpeting in the basement where everyone will be sitting on the floor. I just stayed in my room reading all day.

I'm not going to bhajan because I've decided not to be Indian anymore. I'm going to be completely American from now on. I don't want anyone making fun of me because I'm weird.

As I lie on my bed reading, I hear the front door opening and closing and lots of footsteps in the hallway. I hear loud voices as everyone arrives. I ignore it all and concentrate on my book.

The door to my room bursts open, and Anushri comes in. "Leela, aren't you going to come down and sing a song with me?" At every bhajan, Anushri and I usually lead one of the songs together.

I shake my head. "No, I'm not coming down."

Anushri shrugs and walks out the door. Everything quiets down. I guess everyone is down in the basement singing. I keep reading. I wonder whether

anyone notices that I'm not there. They probably don't. But I don't care.

After a long time, my door opens again. It's Mom.

"Why don't you come down for dinner, at least," she says. "Everyone wants to see you."

I *am* getting hungry. I climb off the bed. I look down at the clothes I'm wearing—pink shorts and a pink T-shirt.

There's a chocolate ice-cream stain on the shirt. I think about changing my clothes before going downstairs but decide not to. Who cares?

There are lots and lots of people downstairs, sitting on the sofas and on the floor. "Hello, Leela!" everyone says. My mother's friends try to give me hugs, but I shrug them away.

All the kids are sitting at a table. As soon as I sit down next to Anushri, she says, "Leela, I just had a great idea! You know how our Girl Scout troop has to pick a country for international day?"

I nod. Anushri continues, "I'm going to ask if our troop can pick India. Ajji can help us! She can come to our next meeting!"

I look at her. "No way," I say.

"Why not?" Anushri asks.

"Crystal's in our troop! She'll make fun of us!"

"So what if she does?" Anushri asks. "I'm not going to let Crystal ruin things for me."

"Well, I don't want Ajji to come to our troop meeting."

"You don't even like Ajji!" Anushri says. "I'm going to ask her anyway."

"Anushri, you can't! She's not your ajji. She's *my* ajji, and I say we shouldn't ask her."

Anushri doesn't say anything.

"Anushri, promise me you won't ask Ajji to come to the Girl Scout meeting."

Finally she says, "Okay."

CHAPTER 6
The Third Eye

On Tuesday after school, Anushri and I go to the school library for our Girl Scout meeting. As I walk through the door, I see something I can't believe. Sitting at one of the tables, right next to our troop leader, Mrs. Fitcher, is Ajji!

I look at Anushri. "You promised that you wouldn't ask Ajji to come here!"

Anushri looks down at her shoes. "I had my fingers crossed." She walks over to Ajji. How could Anushri do this to me?

I know Crystal is going to make fun of Ajji—and me!

After Mrs. Fitcher introduces her, Ajji stands up.

"Today I will teach you about *rangoli*," she says. "These are beautiful patterns that women in India make on the floors of their houses, to welcome the goddess Lakshmi. Traditionally, these designs are made of rice powder."

Ajji takes a bit of rice powder out of a plastic container, holds it between her index finger and thumb, and quickly sprinkles neat lines of the powder onto a piece of black construction paper. Soon we see a pretty pattern of diamonds and loops in the shape of a flower.

"Wow!" the girls gasp.

"I will not ask you to make your designs with rice powder!" Ajji laughs. "I will teach you to draw them with a pen."

"And," Mrs. Fitcher says, "once we learn some designs, we'll make glitter note cards to sell at our international day celebration!"

Ajji shows us how to make a grid of dots and how to use that grid as a guide to create a design. I look around the room. All the girls seem pretty interested in what Ajji is teaching. Even Crystal is watching. Maybe this won't be so bad.

After a while, Mrs. Fitcher leaves to set up our snack in the hallway because we're not allowed to eat in the library. Everyone is bent over pieces of paper, working on creating their designs—everyone but Crystal.

Crystal is sitting across from me. She hasn't drawn anything. In the middle of her forehead is one of those plastic googly eyes. She must have gotten it out of the craft box. Crystal is rolling her eyes and nodding her head to make the googly eye jiggle. She looks silly. But I can't laugh. I feel too embarrassed. I hear a few giggles around me from other girls.

I look at Ajji. She is trying to smile, but her brow is furrowed.

More and more girls are starting to laugh. I look at Anushri, sitting at the other end of the table. I see her chin quiver. Even Anushri, who said she didn't

care about Crystal's teasing, is about to cry! I know I have to do something.

"Take that off right now!" I yell.

Mrs. Fitcher comes back in. "What's going on, girls?" she asks.

The laughter stops. No one says a word. Mrs. Fitcher looks around the room. I sneak a look at Crystal and see that she has removed the googly eye.

"Leela, I heard your voice," Mrs. Fitcher says. "Do you want to tell me why you were yelling like that?" Mrs. Fitcher is glaring at me.

What should I do? I could just refuse to talk. Then maybe everyone will stop staring at me. But if I don't say anything, Crystal will just keep making fun of me.

"Leela, I'm waiting."

Suddenly, I know what I want to do. I take a deep breath. I say, "I yelled because Crystal was making fun of the dot on my grandmother's forehead."

Mrs. Fitcher nods. But I'm not done talking. I continue, "I want to tell everyone why Indian women wear a dot on their foreheads. The dot is called a *kumkum*. People who follow the Hindu religion wear it. Some people say it's like a third eye." I look at Crystal. "But many women wear it because it looks pretty."

"What is it made of?" Lucy asks.

"You can buy a liquid to paint on your forehead," I say. "My ajji actually makes hers out of a powder. She puts a spot of petroleum jelly on her forehead and sticks the red powder to it. But my favorite kind is a self-stick kumkum. You can get kumkums in a lot of different colors, shapes, and sizes. Some of them have jewels or glitter on them."

"Do boys and men wear a kumkum, too?" Sarah asks.

"Yes, but they usually just smear a little bit of red powder on their forehead in the morning, and it gets rubbed off soon. They don't care about making it look pretty."

"Thank you, Leela," Mrs. Fitcher says.

When I pick up my pencil again, my hands are shaking.

After the meeting, Anushri and I help Ajji pack up. "You made a very good speech," Ajji says.

I smile. Then I see Crystal coming over to us. "Need any help?" she asks.

Anushri glares at her.

"We're all set," I say.

Crystal turns to Ajji. "I'm sorry I made fun of your, uh, kumkum."

Ajji puts her hand on Crystal's shoulder.

"Now that you understand why I wear a kumkum, you won't need to make fun anymore."

"Yeah." Crystal smiles and heads out the door.

I look at Ajji. "I can't believe she said she was sorry!"

"I can't believe you said what you did!" Anushri says. "You're so shy about speaking in front of other people. How did you do it?"

I shrug. "I decided you were right. I didn't want to let Crystal ruin things. And I wanted her to understand that Ajji doesn't wear a kumkum to look silly, like Crystal did. She wears it to look pretty."

"So do you still not want to be Indian?" Anushri asks.

I smile. "I guess not. Even though it's sometimes hard to be different, it's also really neat.

"I get to be American and Indian at the same time. I get to do American things, like wearing shorts and eating peanut butter. But I also get to do Indian things, like singing bhajans and eating gulab jamun!"

"Right!" Anushri says.

I look at Ajji and say, "I'm glad you came today to teach us rangoli."

Ajji gives me a hug. "And I'm glad to have my Indian-American granddaughter back!"

Indian Pronunciation Guide

Here is a guide for pronouncing the Indian names and words used in this book.

        ajji: *UJ jee*
      Anushri: *UH noo shree*
  autoriksha: *AW tow RICK shaw*
   Bangalore: *BANG uh loor*
       bhajan: *BUH jun*
     chappals: *CHUP puls*
gulab jamun: *goo LAHB jah MOON*
     Kannada: *KUN nah dah*
     kumkum: *KOOM koom*
      Lakshmi: *LUHK shmee*
        langa: *LUN gah*
        Leela: *LEE lah*
      rangoli: *run GOH lee*
         sari: *SAH ree*